A HISTORY of KNA

KNA
270 Sandycombe Road,
Kew, Richmond, Surrey TW9 3NP

Phone:
020 8948 8054
or
07951 293 319

www.kna.org.uk

twitter:@KNA1977

facebook:@KewNeighbourhood

registered charity number 1034340

KEW • NEIGHBOURHOOD ASSOCIATION

KEW

NEIGHBOURHOOD

ASSOCIATION

2017 Cover page designed by Lyn Keay

A history of KNA
From 1976-1998 by Mary Bonham Carter
and from 1996-2017 by Sue Kirkpatrick

2017 Self-published by the KNA Association   via
www.createspace.com; and is a work of non-fiction.

Available directly from the KNA or from world-wide Amazon sites.

ISBN - 978-1979672979
ISBN - 13 978-1979672979

With thanks to all those involved with KNA past and present.

If you would like to become a KNA volunteer please contact us.

See Page One for details.

CONTENTS

Page

LIST OF PHOTOS AND ILLUSTRATIONS

A Beginning

'HELPING PEOPLE TO HELP PEOPLE'

1976 to 1998 written by Mary Bonham Carter.

On looking back over the last 22 years from the first beginnings of the KNA to the present day it is gratifying to see how well established the organisation has become. Many people have contributed to this success over the years, and it will be inevitable that not everyone can be mentioned in this short history, but without them the KNA would not be here today. It may also be that other people remember the events in another way, however, I have tried my best to write about everything as it happened from the beginning and have had access to all the relevant papers that remain with the group.

Our thanks must go to Tina Wood who took up the idea and set it all in motion.

During the summer of 1976 following a Kew Liberal meeting at the Beehive Pub the idea of a neighbourhood help group was talked about by Tina Wood, Jenny Tonge and myself. The first meeting was held at Tina's home in Maze Road a few weeks later, and she became the first co-ordinator/secretary.

In Kew we had the feeling that there was a gap in community spirit. As new families moved into the area with little support from relatives too far away and elderly people confined at home needed help or contact with local services. With that in mind discussions centred around forming a non-denominational, non-political base for people to communicate with each other. The underlying thinking was that we as a community should be able to support others who were less fortunate or able.

Tina had at first envisaged that each road would have a 'helper' upon whom the residents could call when there was a need, rather like the Neighbourhood Watch scheme which started up later. This 'helper' would have at their fingertips advice of all sorts from plumbers to useful local telephone numbers. Tina had prepared folders containing all the relevant information for each helper and by the end of 1976 we had a core group of helpers of about 10. It was soon obvious that we wouldn't be able to achieve our aim of a representative for each street but we had enough people who were able to provide a contact for those requesting help.

We wanted to include all of Kew and North Sheen, the area bounded by the Kew Road, Lower Mortlake Road, Lower Richmond Road and the River Thames. So the name of Kew and North Sheen Neighbourhood Association was used. This eventually became the Kew Neighbourhood Association, KNA for short. Later in 1992 at the request of the Richmond Parish Lands Charity, our main funding body, the original area was increased to include Manor Road and Clifford Avenue.

Gradually we took on a more formal approach and the Reverend Roger Lamont, who was then the vicar of the Barn Church, agreed to let us have our meetings in his church hall and was prepared to chair those meetings.

Thus our inaugural meeting took place on 3rd October 1976 at the Barn Church and in December the following year we had our First Birthday Party when approximately 50 people attended.

We aimed to have discussions on local matters and during the year a member of the Gingerbread Group talked about one parent families and this highlighted their problem of caring for children while the parent was at work. John Parton gave a talk on 'Environmental Health' illustrating with slides the work of the public health officers.

Another of the first speakers was Colin Stamp, who gave a very interesting account of the start of the Barnes Community Association. They had purchased and renovated an old house, 'Rose Cottage', in Barnes High Street for their headquarters and this provided a 'drop in centre' staffed by volunteers. This seemed ideal for a community venture and although at that time in 1977, KNA explored the possibility for a similar base, the place or funds just weren't available.

The following year, 1978, we hosted an Election Forum in the Barn Church Hall. The three main contenders for the council [David Blomfield (Lib), Serge Lourie (Lab), Crispin Shaddock (Cons)] spoke of their hopes and aims and answered questions. The controversy about the Bail Hostel in North Road attracted many local residents to this meeting.

For a short time a representative from the CAB came one afternoon a week to the Barn Church Hall, the rental at £1 for a session was paid for by KNA. As so few people came for advice, despite a wide distribution of advertising leaflets, we reluctantly discontinued this service.

In September 1978, Ros Buckland Wright became our Secretary, but in reality she was our first co-ordinator and continued the aims of the association to bring together the people needing help and those willing to give help. Ros worked from her own home and managed to juggle this voluntary work with looking after her two young children. I know what an effort this was as after Ros resigned, I took over. Our volunteers were increasing, and so were requests for gardening jobs for which we spent £10 to buy some tools.

On reviewing the requests for help there were many driving trips to hospitals and to dental appointments, one off garden tidying jobs; babysitting (especially for members of the Gingerbread Group); shopping and visiting the elderly. Two requests that Marjorie Barnes well remembers are cleaning up a pensioner's flat in Chilton Road following a fire, and taking a toddler for walks as his mother had both legs in plaster. Ros kept the 'day book' and at the end of her first year noted, amongst our many requests, that we had helped a resident pack up as she was leaving the district and hoped that it bore no reflection on KNA!

Basil Kardasis, lived locally and worked in advertising, and very kindly designed our first logo in July 1980. To this day except for some minor modifications it remains much the same.

The celebrations in 1977 for the Queen's Jubilee included a huge fete on Kew Green. The KNA organised a 'White Elephant' stall and we made a grand profit of £34.54, which then had to be divided between us and the Jubilee Committee. Local improvements funded by other money raised at this fete was the creation of a garden by the side of St. Luke's House, improvements to the forecourt of Kew Gardens Station and an extension to the hut for the Pensioners Bowls Club in the North Sheen Recreation Ground.

As can be seen from the treasurer's report over those early years funds were minimal and by the end of 1977 including money from the Mayor's fund and the local Liberal Recycling Group, we had been given just over £100. During the next few years this increased to about £200 annually.

As the Association was becoming established it was thought that leaflets should be distributed to publicise the help being offered and also to ask for more helpers. At one 'leaflet drop' alone 5,500 leaflets were distributed to every home in the area by our own volunteers and from volunteers of the Townmead Youth Club.

The idea of a monthly Neighbourhood Newspaper was proposed by Alan Campbell early in 1978, but the cost of producing and delivering it just wasn't financially viable. Later in 1987 Nigel Halliday and

Julia Jones did start a newsletter and it went to at least three issues and kept members in touch with community events and the KNA.

Some of the horticultural students at Kew Gardens, who lived at Gumley Cottage, grew their own vegetables and offered their surplus to us which we delivered to the kitchens at Abbeyfields in Ennerdale Road. Possibly organic, definitely most earthy, but excellent carrots, potatoes and cabbages were enjoyed by the residents.

A jumble sale held in 1978 at St. Peter's Hall in Marksbury Avenue (now rebuilt as houses), helped to promote our profile and raise funds of £59.83. Later another jumble sale only brought in 75p! We organised a stall for the KNA at several Richmond May Fayres and sold cakes and jams, again boosting our funds. When Kew revived their own fair in 1988 KNA had a grand display of photographs and a Treasure Hunt map of Kew. Our colours of black and yellow stood out well.

Meals were cooked and taken to needy residents during the public holidays and were especially welcome at Christmas time.

It is of interest to note that in 1978 about 5 young representatives of the "The Moonies" (the World Unification Church) who had come to Kew, were a great help with most of our gardening requests, so much so that quite a back log of these were cleared up. We got to know one member, a very pleasant young girl who helped many residents, babysitting etc. These Moonies who had come from the States lived with families in Kew paying their way, and at the end of their summer stay they asked all the people they had got to know to attend a rally at Olympia. It was some years later that the leader of this sect, Sun Yat Moon, was exposed, but even then we wondered what it was that held them to this way of life. Their stay in England was surely meant to be a recruiting effort to find more members for their cult, and although their help for the KNA was much appreciated I don't think the citizens of Kew were tempted to join the Moonies. There were no repercussions thank goodness.

Requests for help slowly began to increase. During those first years volunteers took it in turns to have the Day Book at their home and in this was recorded every phone call and the type of help needed and the person who gave that help. Some of us had small children and requests would inevitably come through at the end of an afternoon when one was busiest, so juggling family life with neighbourliness took some skill and patience.

St. Luke's school house in Sandycombe Road had been renovated and became a Community Centre and in 1982 our funds enabled us to part rent the music room and we shared this with a piano. When in 1990 a separate room became available we then had our own office at St. Luke's. A volunteer was there every morning during the week, and for a short while we had a shift on Wednesday evenings because most volunteers were at home then and could be more readily contacted.

Because of the activities of KNA many helpers had taken on one client with whom they arranged to shop or drive on a regular basis. By 1988 there were 17 Befrienders on our list and Melanie Hughes co-ordinated this group.

A social group was also set up with about 20 younger members they were organised by Hazel Jewell, and would meet regularly at a pub. Between them they were also able to help people on behalf of KNA.

In 1987 Richmond Council were housing homeless families in bed and breakfast accommodation in Kew. During the day these families roamed the streets with nowhere to go or anywhere to eat. The Barn Church very kindly loaned their kitchen to be manned by KNA volunteers so that these families could prepare meals for their children, and this continued until Richmond Council found proper housing for these families. Eva Tendler was especially concerned because she felt that not only were these children being deprived of a settled home life but very often they were missing out on schooling.

The Pushers, started in 1987, but their name was soon changed to 'The Wheelie Club' for obvious reasons. Caroline Sheldon was the originator and organiser and for some years a weekly afternoon outing was arranged for volunteers to take people in their wheelchairs around Kew Gardens. This gave a great deal of pleasure to many housebound and frail clients of KNA. It was pressure from KNA, arising out of problems encountered by our wheelers, which brought about a change of rules at Kew Gardens, and they now permit entry for a wheelchair occupant and their 'pusher' for a single entrance fee. In 1992 KNA bought their own wheelchair.

Prompted perhaps by these successful outings a picnic was organised in Kew Gardens to bring together everyone involved in KNA. Held in June in 1987 more than 80 people attended and it was of especial enjoyment and benefit to the elderly and lonely.

Volunteer week in June 1987 spurred us arrange a stall outside Barclays Bank at Kew Station to attract more helpers. Jenny Tonge lent us her yellow landrover and to the tune of 'Neighbours' wafting around the streets of Kew each morning, Hazel Jewell was heard speaking through a loudspeaker encouraging people to join KNA. At the end of the week Barbara Purvis collated an information leaflet for newcomers to Kew and this was distributed widely. Over the borough KNA won the 'gold star' for recruiting the most volunteers, obviously 'neighbours' did the trick.

Zig Nowicki, a social worker, joined us in 1990 as co-ordinator. He organised meetings regularly with the helpers and formed a committee of local people. This began to consolidate KNA into a more efficiently run group. The office was open every week day morning and staffed by a regular group of 10 volunteers.

Jim Thomas was Chairman from 1991 to 95 and was very ably helped by Ros Poland, vice chair. Ros had come to live in Kew in 1985 and almost at once became a very active supporter. She remembered that she came to the first real AGM in 1986. Many meetings of the office group were held at her house in Alexandra Road and with coffee, biscuits and cake the mornings passed all too quickly in a most friendly way.

By 1994 statistics show that we had about 160 clients and 200 helpers, over that year the number of jobs completed would have been well over three thousand. Peggy Thompson and Susan Robinson were always on hand to drive until they themselves could no longer do this. There were also the three musketeers: so called because they were always available for any last minute driving jobs and must have clocked up thousands of miles between them, Fred Morgan, Buster Manley and Vic Weber.

Through a generous donation of £5,000 a scheme was set up to pay for a carer to give a relative respite from caring for a relative at night. Despite every effort this scheme was not taken up. The donor, who wished to remain anonymous, generously agreed for this money to be used for providing care-lines. This is an alarm used for the elderly and infirm and placed around their neck. If they should fall and need help they can press the alarm to alert central control. In 1994 there were eight in use. Kew Carer's Relief managed by KNA received a donation of £1,000 from the McKenna Foundation in 1994. This provided funding for 5 care-lines with the RPLC funding another 5.

By 1994 RPLC were giving us a grant of £7,300 and had also funded the cost of a computer for the co-ordinator. Richmond Borough gave us a grant for £1,250. The CVS paid for all the mileage that the volunteers did and reimbursed them monthly.

The Kew Neighbourhood Association was started by a few in the early days with an enthusiasm to promote a caring society. It has grown, incorporating many different ideas and able to care for more people, into a well-run organisation mostly funded by the RPLC.

1980s Mary Bonham Carter and Tina Wood.

List of Offices held

CHAIR

Roger Lamont	1977-78
Nigel Halliday	1986-88
Chris Yellowly	1988-91
Jim Thomas	1991-95
Liz Harris	1995

VICE CHAIR

Yvonne Abbatt	1986-90
Ros Poland	1990-96
Jane Spence	1996

CO-ORDINATOR - SECRETARY

Tina Wood	1976-78
Joyce Rodgers	1977-82
Ros BucklandWright	1978-79
Mary BonhamCarter	1979-85
Julia Jones	1986-88
Penelope Harrison	1988-90
Zig Nowicki	1990-2003

TREASURER

Marjorie Barnes	1977-78
Mary BonhamCarter	1982-88
Liz Harris	1988-94
Josie Adams	1994-99

From 1976 to 1994 - Resume

1976   Beginnings at the Beehive Pub in Popham Gardens (now a block of flats)

Accounts kept - donations from local residents, Liberal Recycling Group and from the Mayor's Fund - £100.

1977   Affiliation with Council for Voluntary Service.

1982   Rental of office and use of telephone at St. Luke's House

1985   Our own telephone line installed.

Reimbursement of money for petrol used by drivers from CVS.

1986   First paid co-ordinator (Julia Jones) 15 hours per week at £5 per hour

Constitution adopted and boundaries defined for KNA as those of Kew Ward.

First grant from Richmond Borough (applied for by Angela Ball) of £1,113.

First grant from Richmond Parish Lands Charity of £2,000.

Donation from the Richmond Mayor's Fund £450

1988   Grant from Richmond Borough £1,100

1989   Moved into larger office, with sole use, at St. Luke's House, rent of £483 pa.

1990   Third co-ordinator (Zig Nowicki, a Senior Social Worker) 16 hours per week.

Barbara Purvis compiled Directory for Newcomers to Kew (updated 1993)

1991   Minicab scheme. RPLC funded cost for clients use of a minicab returning from hospital appointments.

1992   At RPLC's request the KNA area was extended south to include boundaries of Manor Road the railway and Clifford Avenue.

New constitution adopted – draft prepared by Dick Poland.

1993   Charitable status applied for by Jim Thomas

Amendments to constitution requested by Charity Commissioners was agreed.

1994   Charitable status granted. No: 1034340.

Rent paid to SLH £483 p.a.

Yearly Numbers of Requests from 1987-1998

Year	Requests for help	Clients	Volunteers
1987			105
1992	573	160	200
1993	694		
1994	724	134	128
1995	749	150	100
1996	2400	166	100
1997	2280	150	129
1998	2263	135	130

And so towards the Millenium, it is wonderful to know that KNA is thriving in the community and liaising with other groups and continues to be of great use to the residents of Kew, not only that but is using the new technology that inevitably is now part of our lives.

Mary Bonham Carter

........AND 20 YEARS ON

By Sue Kirkpatrick

Kew Neighbourhood Association was granted charitable status in 1994 under the watch of Jim Thomas as Chair and Zig Nowicki as Co-ordinator. Registered number: 1034340. The objectives of the Charity "are to provide services and facilities for the elderly, disabled, mentally or physically handicapped, the sick and those suffering hardship".

The policies adopted in order to achieve these objectives are to provide transport for visits to the local community centre/ hospitals/ clinics/doctors/dentists and rehab clinics as well as shopping, befriending and light gardening.

The geographical boundaries are pretty much what people would define as the area within the London Borough of Richmond upon Thames known as Kew, bordered by the three main roads, Kew Road leading up to the Richmond Circus roundabout, the Mortlake Road and the A316 (Lower Mortlake Road and Lower Richmond Roads), with a few roads historically included on the other side of the A316 around the Sainsbury's supermarket area.

The Charity is managed by a Committee of Trustees with the day to day business run by a paid part-time Co-ordinator, currently Abi Palmer, and a very large number of volunteers. Volunteers work as drivers, in the office doing the administrative work of connecting drivers with driving jobs needed, as befrienders and/or helping with shopping and gardening. They also move in and out of different roles on the Committee, e.g. the current Chair of the Board of Trustees is also an active driver, as have been other Chairs and several Treasurers. Many of the volunteers have been involved for a great number of years and some for so long that they have indeed moved on from being volunteers to being recipients of a service themselves. A completing of the circle of hands.

1996 to 2017 written by Sue Kirkpatrick.

Mary Bonham Carter who wrote the KNA history from its inception until 1996 retired in 1996, as did Ros Poland who had been very involved. During the next five years the core business of driving clients continued and new initiatives were started. The Annual General Meeting of 1998 noted that 1494 driving jobs had been undertaken as well as 725 non-driving jobs and the number of volunteers stood at 130.

The Co-ordinator at this time was Zig Nowicki, with Liz Harris and then David Fasken Chairs of the Board of Trustees.

Squires had agreed to deliver shopping to clients unable to get out. KNA was anxious to develop its shopping service but was receiving little response from its enquiries to Social Services to help with identifying need.

Volunteers were noticing that requests for driving to hospitals was beginning to include hospitals some distance away from Kew, e.g. St George's in Tooting, and this trend has continued.

Regular meetings for the office volunteers were started in this period and they continue to-day. Office volunteers work on their own for two+ hours each weekday morning, matching clients' requests for transport to volunteers able to do the jobs. It is helpful to be able to meet on a six/eight weekly basis to share any problems and concerns.

A very significant change in 1999 was the closure of the Council's Social Services- run Day Centre for older people in St Luke's (what is now the Avenue Club). There was much concern in Kew about what alternative provision could be made for Kew residents as the nearest Social Services provision would then be at premises in East Sheen. The Day Centre at that time had 160 members but these would not have been all Kew residents.

In the event, and as a result of much local lobbying, the Day Centre was replaced by what is now the Avenue Club run by Kew

Community Trust and this seems to have become remarkably successful very quickly and continues to be so. (The history of Kew Community Trust and the Avenue Club was published in October 2017).

From KNA's perspective the opening of the Avenue Club posed a bit of a challenge as Zig Nowicki was concerned that volunteers would be over-run with requests for transport to the club. Initially KNA agreed only to transport people wanting hairdressing or chiropody. There was a view that KNA should not be asked to undertake a service that should more properly be done by Social Services. However, it soon became clear that Social Services had no intention of providing this. By 2001 the Avenue Club had become an extremely successful social club providing a wide range of different activities, including outings, as well as lunch and refreshments at very reasonable cost. Transporting clients to the club soon became a core part of KNA's workload.

1996 saw the first of what became annual volunteer get-togethers, at first in the home of Liz Harris, with drinks and nibbles, eventually moving in 2001 to a rather larger annual party at St Winifred's Church Hall organised and funded by Committee members. These were held after the Annual General Meeting.

1998 saw the first "coffee morning" organised for clients; this swiftly became an annual tea party at the Avenue Club which, with the exception of a couple of anniversary years, has become a regular annual fixture. In early years sandwiches and cakes would be provided by volunteers but in more recent times, with KNA finances in better shape, the tea is now "bought in" with volunteers serving and transporting. Some form of entertainment is also always provided and the current Mayor usually puts in an appearance. Inevitably some more entertaining than others; there was the year when it was thought that sharing out banjos and getting the clients to learn a simple tune would be a good idea. As a degree of deafness is not unknown amongst older people those at the back were usually out of step and arthritic hands do not lend themselves easily to the plucking of strings!

The distribution of Harvest Festival parcels by Broomfield School was started in 1996/97 by Nada Morgan, then a teacher at the school. Nada recalls a story of walking with some children to deliver parcels when they passed a church where a funeral had just finished. One child asked what the gathering was about and, on being told, remarked "Oh dear, she hasn't had her parcel"! The parcels continue to be delivered by the school to-day, KNA's involvement being to supply the names of clients who would like them.

The AGM of 2001 noted that there were 169 clients with 85 volunteers, a big increase in clients due to the increased commitment to taking people to the Avenue Club.

During these five years funding continued to come mainly from grants from the Council and from Richmond Parish Lands Charity, together with donations from local businesses and individuals. There was a significant donation from Sam Newton to provide social activities for clients which could include financial help to the Avenue Club.

2003-2010

In 2003 Zig Nowicki retired, as did the then Chair Jenny Powell-Smith. Zig had been a significant influence on the development of KNA as not only was he a very outgoing and enthusiastic Co-ordinator but he was also a professional social work manager with many years' experience of working for a local authority.

The roles were taken over by Janet McAllister as Co-ordinator and Joan Brown as Chair, with Derrick Schauerman as Treasurer. All three were new to the task and they did an excellent job in keeping everything together. Derrick was particularly active in raising funds for KNA via the Richmond Philanthropic Society.

An early but ongoing task starting in 2004 was to achieve a functioning computer system which could facilitate the day-to-day management of matching jobs to clients as well as producing quickly the data needed for the Co-ordinator to provide accountability both to the Trustees and to the funding bodies. The early system at this stage was primarily for data collection; the office volunteers were still managing the day-to-day work using paper records which was time consuming and could not easily be consulted outside office hours.

The 2003 AGM noted that there were 166 clients and 77 volunteers with 1557 driving and 588 non driving jobs having been completed. The core driving jobs continued to be stable, to the Avenue Club, GPs, hospitals, dentists, rehab clinics, hairdressing, chiropody, shopping and non-driving jobs at this time was primarily gardening.

Joan Brown commented "there was always a representative from one of the local churches on the Board of Trustees and this was useful as they were in a good position to know which of their parishioners might be needing help with transport." This representation continues to this day. Joan also noted "office volunteers were expected to train each other on the paper system with help from the Chair and driver volunteers were expected to find at least one client each".

By 2005 Rea Granleese had been working hard to drum up donations from local businesses, together with prizes for the raffles at the clients' annual parties. Priory Management which is run by Rea Granleese's wife continues to make an annual donation as do other local businesses and individuals. Rea remembers driving people way back at the start of KNA when he would be given chocolates or homemade marmalade because he was "such a nice young man". Rea considers that it is important to have good PR, to put in the work "knocking on doors" and to form a relationship with donors. He became the semi-official KNA fundraiser, which task he has been performing excellently until very recently.

It is important to acknowledge that there are also many one-off donations from individuals, all of which, large or small, are most gratefully received in helping to keep KNA afloat.

2005 also saw the start of the Sainsburys shopping bus, as well as the 80% taxi fare reimbursement from hospital appointments back home, funded by the RPLC.

In 2006 the need to take up references for volunteer drivers started. At that time Disclosure and Barring Service (DBS, then known as CRB) checks were only required for befrienders who would be going into people's homes but this changed the following year when all volunteers who had any direct contact with clients were required to have checks. Occasionally these checks have taken considerable time (typically in relation to people who have recently moved, especially from abroad) and some potential volunteers may have been lost in the process; however, most have accepted with equanimity and forbearance that we live in changing times and the current processing is generally faster.

2007 saw the 30th anniversary of KNA. A splendid afternoon was put on for the clients, starting with a tea party at the Botanist restaurant on Kew Green and finishing with a train ride around Kew Gardens. This afternoon was made possible by additional funding from Priory Management.

In 2008 Bill Timmis, who was Treasurer at the time, put much effort into formalising the accounts in a simple way. This was essential because of the increased scrutiny being given to how grants were used and moves to annual applications for funding. Readers will note that Bill Timmis later became Chair and until very recently, has continued to drive for KNA, a good example of how a great many volunteers have undertaken different roles over the years.

2009 was the year when KNA first attended Kew Sparkle, the annual Christmas Fair in early December, to both promote the service and raise funds. The huge and magnificent Christmas cake, which goes to the person who has come closest to guessing its correct weight, has for many years been made by Jean Dorman and iced by Frances Leach. Guessing the number of sweets in an outsize jar has also always been very popular with the children.

The KNA volunteer's stal

From left

Jean Dorman Joan Brown Frances Leach

2010-2017

In 2010 Joan Brown stood down as Chair and was replaced by Jean Dorman.

In the office Jean put in a great deal of time with Janet McAllister transferring all the hand written client details onto the computer. A new system then allowed the office volunteers to manage the referral of new jobs and matching jobs to volunteer drivers on line rather than the more labour- intensive paper system that had been in place previously. Janet had good computer skills and Jean endless drive so that between them, and with some outside help from an IT professional, they managed to get a workable computer system up and running.

2010 was the first year that KNA attended the annual Kew Mid-Summer Fete, at which KNA has had a presence ever since, another good opportunity to promote KNA, attract more volunteers and encourage residents to consider any neighbours who might like some help. On these occasions, Sarah's Game is a good fund-raiser, a game of chance (the chance of winning £20 for an outlay of £1 or £50 for an outlay of £2 - irresistible) which has been provided for many years by Sarah Hodgson. Mini golf also proves popular.

Caroline Smee organised a very successful charity tennis tournament and lunch at Pensford Tennis Club. She writes "we made mountains of coronation chicken and salads. Puddings came courtesy of Costco though we didn't tell anyone this! We had received some very generous donations of raffle prizes for which we sold tickets mercilessly. There was even a competition during and after lunch to measure the speed of your serve at £1 a go which brought out the competitive spirit in many. At the end of a long and enjoyable day £1,000 had been raised for KNA".

This was the first year that parties for volunteers began to be held in the homes of the current Chair with rather more substantial nibbles and unlimited wine. There has been some concern expressed about whether this annual duty might deter people from offering to stand as Chairs but so far this doesn't seem to have happened!

A paper newsletter for KNA clients and volunteers was started but not continued, possibly because of the time needed to produce it and/or the development of social media forums. Wider use of e-mails now makes it possible to contact most volunteers.

The 35th Anniversary Party took place in 2012 at the Musical Museum in Brentford, with celebrity guest Judith Chalmers. Clients were taken there in mini-buses driven by David Polya from the Avenue Club and Andrew Brown, KNA volunteer and Trustee. The Mighty Wurlitzer was played and the party was a huge success, much enjoyed by all who attended.

Befriending had been happening in a small way in the earlier years of KNA. The "Wheelie Club" was started by Caroline Sheldon in 1987 to take people in wheelchairs around Kew Gardens but this stopped when Caroline left Kew. Melany Hughes was also involved in organising some befriending in the earlier years but, again, this seems not to have survived her departure from Kew.

Some befriending in Kew was organised by Janet and Jean on a fairly ad hoc and limited basis due to shortage of time. The Richmond Consortium, a group of local voluntary bodies, had been started around this time and had appointed a "Befriending Co-ordinator" but there seemed to be few referrals coming from Kew. This post finally folded and responsibility for local befriending was passed back to KNA.

As the KNA Co-ordinator did not have the time and there was no local volunteer who came forward to promote it, in 2011 Michael Hill was asked by Jean Dorman if he could help KNA with leaflets. Coming from a background in publicity, Michael had been working with the Richmond Consortium. Soon after, he was appointed on a part-time basis to take forward befriending in Kew.

Michael notes that it was slow to get started with not a great many referrals, possibly because Kew is already a very community minded area. Currently there are 19 active matches.

This period is also notable for a very large donation (bequest) from the estate of local resident Joan Blackwell which has made a significant and continuing difference to KNA's financial security. It has enabled the charity to be freed up from some of the day-to-day concerns about income generation to focus on more developmental work, such as the planned expansion of befriending and a more effective computer system (as mentioned below).

For Richmond Council's commissioning purposes KNA is now in a "hub" currently managed by INS (Integrated Neurological Services) and referred to as a CILS (Community Independent Living Service); at present KNA is a non-contracted member and therefore can maintain a greater degree of independence.

In 2014 Janet McAllister retired and the current Co-ordinator Abi Palmer was appointed. Jean Dorman also stepped down after several years as Chair and was succeeded by Bill Timmis. Bill commented "KNA is an excellent small charity, with the office volunteers as the backbone and the volunteer drivers as essential. It is important to work closely with the Avenue Club but not to merge completely with it as this could result in a loss of individuality for KNA."

In 2014/15 KNA had 104 volunteers and 135 active clients. Ongoing funding continues to be provided by annual grants from Richmond Council and from Richmond Parish Lands Charity, as well as donations from individuals, local businesses, the First Friday Lunch at St Winifred's Church, Kew Rotary, Kew Fete, Kew Sparkle, Kew Village Market and other fundraising organisations who donate their proceeds to different charities in the area. KNA also fundraises on its own behalf at local events.

Chris Evans Appleyard Companion Co-ordinator(left) Abi Palmer
Co-ordinator (right)

A new computer system has been established and all the office
volunteers trained to use it. This makes it much easier for Abi Palmer
to access the increasing amount of data she needs to provide both to
Trustees and to funding bodies.

Harvest Festival parcels continue to be delivered to around 50 people
every year.

Martin Cross receiving a cheque from Kew Market

Bill was in turn succeeded in 2015 by Martin Cross, who is also a volunteer driver for KNA and was a diligent and supportive Chair.

Under Martin's watch, the period from 2015 until 2017 saw several new initiatives. Birthday and Christmas cards are now sent to every KNA client. These are usually delivered by Iain Mulligan who has also been providing gardening help for many years. Feedback from clients indicates that these cards are always much appreciated, as is the gardening.

Visits to clients who expressed an interest were undertaken over two Christmas/New Year periods when the office was closed but there were no requests for this over Christmas 2016 which perhaps needs further exploration in the context of the companionship programme.

A more creative investment of moneys in ethical equity funds rather than deposit accounts, set up by Treasurer Peter Cozens, has increased both capital and income from the Joan Blackwell bequest.

KNA benefited substantially from being chosen as the charity supported by Kew Sparkle at Christmas 2016.

Perhaps the greatest initiative during the past two years was the undertaking of a Loneliness & Social Connections Peer Research Project in Kew, led by Chrysalis Research Consultancy, commissioned by the befriending sub-committee. Thirty two residents over the age of 65 shared their views with ten peer researchers of similar age. This research came up with several recommendations, including "to reach out to different groups of older people who may ordinarily be put off by signing up to a befriending service but would appreciate social contact for a different reason".

As a result, funding has been provided by RPLC for a period of two years to develop a "KNA Companionship Scheme.....addressing loneliness and isolation for Kew's older people by developing ad hoc social connections.......a flexible scheme focussed on doing shared interests and activities together, governed by the individual and the volunteer". Part of the funding is being used to employ a second part-time Co-ordinator with the above brief. This is an ambitious project with the aim of increasing the number of clients who can benefit from companionship in one form or another, but with the traditional one-to-one visits to clients at home remaining.

A befriending sub-committee had been established in 2014 chaired by Alan Jones and, although Alan is no longer involved and the sub-committee now in abeyance, this remains work in progress.

2017 Andrew Brown Chair

Andrew Brown succeeded Martin Cross as Chair in 2017.

With the appointment of the new Companionship Co-ordinator, Chris Evans Appleyard, in June 2017, Michael Hill retired from his work on befriending.

There has been a one off party for volunteers who befriend as well as their being able to attend the general volunteer parties and this is an excellent way for all volunteers to share experiences, problems or successes.

Other current plans include the increased use of social media and improvements to the KNA website, a new leaflet and special events for both clients and volunteers to mark the 40th Anniversary. Possibly short video clips made of volunteers talking to clients about what have often been fascinating lives, demonstrating the mutually-enriching benefits of voluntary activity for both parties.

Summer Party 40 years on

Volunteers waiting in Wheelchairs - Derek Wright, Rick Warden,
Alan Sandall, John Mortley, Ian Harrison

L to r Audrey Wright, Nada Morgan, Joan Dunk,
Patricia Maxwell, Teresa Hartley.

The latest figures at July 2017 show that 2400 driving jobs had been undertaken in 2016 (around 50 per week) with KNA having 80 drivers, 20 shoppers, many of whom also do other driving and two gardeners. There are 11 office volunteers. The number of clients was 189.

2017 KNA Office Volunteers meeting

L to R
Joan Dunk, Sarah Hodgson, Sue Kirkpatrick, Val Kiely, Audrey Wright, Jenny Cross, Sue Phillips.

Those not at the meeting include: Sadie Brooks, Wendy Heubner, Joan Brown, Nicki Edwards.

Throughout the past 20 years there has been ongoing concern about whether KNA could attract enough volunteers to keep the service going. This continues to be a concern as older, very long standing volunteers retire. The earlier concerns about whether the charity could survive financially are now less present due to the very substantial donation made in 2011.

More recently there has been a decrease in the number of jobs to the Avenue Club. One can speculate on why this might be but overall there is no significant diminishing of requests for driving.

So this is very much a Kew charity, started as an idea in a pub in 1976, a service run for Kew residents by mainly Kew people, a tiny but remarkably resilient organisation. It has been able to keep up with some very significant changes over the years where a number of other small charities have foundered; the withdrawal of many Local Authority services for older people, requirements for increasingly stringent accountability and scrutiny in applications for funding, changing local demography, the need for DBS (Disclosure and Barring) checks for all volunteers who have direct contact with clients; huge increase in local traffic with concomitant difficulties in parking etc.

It would be impracticable to try to name each and every volunteer who has played a part in making KNA such a success since its inception. Many go back a very long way indeed and have grown older along with the charity, while others are more recent. Suffice to say that enormous thanks go to all of them, in whatever role, who give their time so generously to ensure that Kew can be a place where the word neighbourhood has real meaning.

And so we look forward to the next 20 years - and beyond....................

Sue Kirkpatrick (on behalf of KNA)
Office volunteer and Trustee

Co-ordinators

1991-2003	Zig Nowicki
2003-2014	Janet McAllister
2014 -	Abi Palmer

Chairpersons

1996-2000	Liz Harris
2000-2002	David Fasken
2002-2003	Jenny Powell-Smith
2003-2010	Joan Brown
2010-2014	Jean Dorman
2014-2015	Bill Timmis
2015-2017	Martin Cross
2017 -	Andrew Brown

Treasurers

1995-1999	Josie Adams
1999-2002	Janet Chesterton
2002-2008	Derrick Schauerman
2008-2013	Bill Timmis
2014-2017	Peter Cozens
2017 -	Josie Adams

A few comments from users and volunteers:

Peter Sainty

Peter Sainty, long standing volunteer with his wife, now both use the service. "Remarkable and useful local service. What would we do without it?"

Dolly Bond

Dolly Bond: "If it wasn't for them I don't know how I would get here. I can't thank them enough, otherwise I'd be housebound."

Kathleen Watkins.
"You're absolutely wonderful. Without you we'd be lost."

Cecile Channon, driver.
" I enjoy doing the volunteer driving, it gets me out. I enjoy having the personal contact and hearing the history of some of our users who were born and have lived all their lives in Kew".

Janet Hicks

"I like coming here (Avenue Club) and the transport is very good".

Jennai Cotterill. "KNA are indispensable. I could not do as many courses if not for KNA. Brilliant, reliable, friendly people".

Sarah Hodgson (driver) with Audrey Miller

Audrey Miller: "I'm very grateful to the people who give up their time, very nice people and easy to talk to. I used to walk here but couldn't come now without the lifts".

Sarah Hodgson, volunteer driver: "It gives me an insight into other people's lives, I enjoy it, you hear some extraordinary things. I was driving one old lady of 97 and we found we had both lived in the same house in Chelsea many years ago. It's very satisfying because I feel I'm giving something back to society, it makes me feel that I'm still useful and have a role. If I'm taking people to hospital talking takes their mind off their appointment and lightens the mood.....I'm like a sponge, a listener, particularly as many are very isolated".

Lisa (Avenue Club Manager). "KNA is a lifeline for many of our older members who would otherwise not be able to get here to enjoy, for instance, gentle exercises, choir, art, knit & stitch, bingo, hairdresser, chiropody, lunch. It enables them to socialise, make friends and avoid being isolated at home. The Avenue Club has always had a good supportive relationship with the KNA office staff and drivers".

Janet Morgans, companion/befriender.

"I enjoy the company of older people, they're all such interesting people and I like hearing about their often fascinating lives. The person I visit also likes to hear about what I am doing. I would really recommend this to other people, it is enjoyable and makes you feel useful".

Printed in Great Britain
by Amazon

40552024R00026